THE STRANGE HOURS TRAVELERS KEEP

AUGUST KLEINZAHLER

The Strange Hours Travelers Keep

faber and faber

First published in the USA in 2003
by Farrar, Straus and Giroux
First published in Great Britain in 2004
by Faber and Faber Limited
3 Queen Square London WC1N 3AU

Typeset by Wilmerset Ltd, Birkenhead, Wirral
Printed in England by T. J. International Ltd, Padstow, Cornwall

A CIP record for this book
is available from the British Library

ISBN 0-571-22173-4

10 9 8 7 6 5 4 3 2 1

For William Corbett of Boston's South End –
friend, poet, friend of poetry

Acknowledgements

Some of these poems appeared in *Agenda*, *Berlin Journal*, *Birdsuit*, *Critical Quarterly*, *Fulcrum*, *Heat*, *London Review of Books*, *Poetry* (Chicago), *The New York Times Book Review*, *Pressed Wafer* and *The Threepenny Review*.

The author wishes to thank the American Academy in Berlin for their hospitality, encouragement and schnapps in the fall of 2000.

Contents

I have discovered that most of
the beauties of travel are due to
the strange hours we keep to see them
William Carlos Williams, 'January Morning'

I had a sentiment for going from here to there
Willem de Kooning

. . . a darling walk for the mind
Robert Burns

THE STRANGE HOURS TRAVELERS KEEP

The Strange Hours Travelers Keep

The markets never rest
Always they are somewhere in agitation
Pork bellies, titanium, winter wheat
Electromagnetic ether peppered with photons
Treasure spewing from Unisys A-15 J mainframes
Across the firmament
Soundlessly among the thunderheads and passenger jets
As they make their nightlong journeys
Across the oceans and steppes

Nebulae, incandescent frog spawn of information
Trembling in the claw of Scorpio
Not an instant, then shooting away
Like an enormous cloud of starlings

Garbage scows move slowly down the estuary
The lights of the airport pulse in morning darkness
Food trucks, propane, tortured hearts
The reticent epistemologist parks
Gets out, checks the curb, reparks
Thunder of jets
Peristalsis of great capitals

How pretty in her tartan scarf
Her ruminative frown
Ambiguity and Reason
Locked in a slow, ferocious tango
Of *if not, why not*

The Old Poet, Dying

He looks eerily young,
what's left of him,
purged, somehow, back into boyhood.
It is difficult not to watch
the movie on TV at the foot of his bed,
40″ color screen,
a jailhouse dolly psychodrama:
truncheons and dirty shower scenes.
I recognize one of the actresses,
now a famous lesbian,
clearly an early B-movie role.
The black nurse says 'Oh dear'
during the beatings.
– *TV in this town is crap*, he says.
His voice is very faint.
He leans toward me,
sliding further and further,
until the nurse has to straighten him out,
scolding him gently.
He reaches out for my hand.
The sudden intimacy rattles me.
He is telling a story.
Two, actually,
and at some point they blend together.
There are rivers and trains,
Oxford and a town near Hamburg.
Also, the night train to Milan
and a lovely Italian breakfast.
The river in Oxford –
he can't remember the name;
but the birds and fritillaria in bloom...
He remembers the purple flowers
and a plate of gingerbread cookies
set out at one of the colleges.

He gasps to remember those cookies.
How surprised he must have been
by the largesse,
and hungry, too,
– *He's drifting in and out*:
I can hear the nurse
on the phone in the other room.
He has been remembering Europe for me.
Exhausted, he lies quiet for a time.
– *There's nothing better than a good pee*,
he says and begins to fade.
He seems very close to death.
Perhaps in a moment, perhaps a week.
Then awakes.
Every patch of story, no matter how fuddled,
resolves into a drollery.
He will perish, I imagine,
en route to a drollery.

Although his poems,
little kinetic snapshots of trees and light,
so denuded of personality
and delicately made
that irony of any sort
would stand out
like a pile of steaming cow flop
on a parquet floor.
We are in a great metropolis
that rises heroically from the American prairie:
a baronial home,
the finest of neighborhoods,
its broad streets nearly empty
on a Saturday afternoon,
here and there a redbud in bloom.
Even in health,
a man so modest and soft-spoken

as to be invisible
among others, in a room almost any size.
It was, I think, a kind of hardship.
– *Have you met what's-his-name yet?*
he asks.
　　　　You know who I mean,
the big shot.
　　　　　　– *Yes*, I tell him, *I have.*
– *You know that poem of his?*
Everyone knows that poem
where he's sitting indoors by the fire
and it's snowing outside
and he suddenly feels a snowflake
on his wrist?
He pauses and begins to nod off.
I remember now the name of the river
he was after, the Cherwell,
with its naked dons, The Parson's Pleasure.
There's a fiercesome catfight
on the TV, with blondie catching hell
from the chicana.
He comes round again and turns to me,
leaning close,
　　　　　　– *Well, of course*, he says,
taking my hand,
his eyes narrowing with malice and delight:
That's not going to be just any old snowflake,
now, is it?

The Swimmer

FOR BRIGHDE

The Japonica and laurels tremble
as the wind picks up
out the west-facing wall of the old natatorium,
made wholly of glass.
The swimmer takes her laps,
steady and sure through a blur of turquoise
and importunings of chlorine.
The large room itself now darkens,
lit as it is by natural light,
as the storm clouds press closer toward land.

Back and forth, the solitary swimmer,
now on her second mile,
is caught up, held almost,
in that one element she finds her ease;
and in moving through it
the very edges of her strength engaged,
until, on a turn, her breathing stretched,
health pours into her.

The great glass wall, first pilloried by drops,
their dull, pellet-like clack,
is now streaming with rain:
and from this hill,
where, half-hidden, the old rec center sits,
across the sixty rolling blocks to the sea,
all that is material and solid,
the houses, the cars, the trees,
diminish into shadow
and continue to recede till there is nothing,
nothing at all in the world,
but water.

A Beautiful Mind

We pushed a tiny catheter and shunt
right through what looked to be a 'propitious bump'
on the skull and into the left hemisphere
of the frontal lobe, way back there,
right above the Sylvian fissure, in the speech area.
And went in again, a long reacher,
all the way back in the temporal lobe,
further along that same stretch of crease,
just behind the ear
and snug up under the collateral sulcus.
Then jerry-rigged a causeway of sorts between them.

You can imagine the mess
and attendant motor disturbances –
flashing lights, dogs barking, sirens.
Like I knew what I was doing, right?
Well, call it two parts dowsing, five parts backhoe.
It was Murph lent me his putty knife;
that is, after I dropped my own.
Ran into a patch of static electricity down there
just about made my hair stand on end.

What I had in mind – *arrrgh, arrrgh* –
was something along the lines of stereophonic sound,
except with words, and more like *wraparound*.
What you might call synergy-enhancement surgery,
one language center communing with another:
Dr Broca, meet Dr Wernicke, like so,
but in new, multiple and unforeseen ways.

Sure, the two had their voltage-gated ion channels,
their desultory whispered chitchats,
Post-it notes along the connective fibers.
But you've seen the flow diagrams: paltry, niggling stuff.

[8]

I've had it with all that,
the parsimonious back and forth between X and Y,
like an insufferably long, indirect taxi ride
between Waterloo Station and West Finchley.
I'm talking time, tedium, the bludgeoning expense.

So I drop down in there with my Davey lamp,
lay down some cable, have a good look-see.
Mercy, Miss Percy, it's worse than the back of your TV.
Might as well have left the trepan set at home.
Never seen anything like it, I tell you what.
Press down there, the eyes start tearing;
down back in there, the willie jumps up and you turn beet red.
Messing about, you can imagine what happens next:

> *Your blistering corolla's ventriloquisms*

> *Sepulveda, der phu-duh-duh*
> > *Knell, wet stencil*
> *Ocarina thirst*

All of that digging only to arrive in Hell:
an endless tape-loop of the aphasic's broken rant,
Friday night forever in the Indeterminists' Revival Tent.

Across the Land

Green rising off the black monster earth
Lolling gourds
Oak limbs snapping in a freak early snow
Redbird and goldfinch glinting across it
Low, over the fast-shadowing ground

What I can't seem to get past
Is the school band's September rehearsals
The tubas, drums and clarinets
Carrying our way from a distant field
The good beefy children playing their hearts out
Braids, buttons and epaulets
In that heat
American as cleanser, as 1958

Do you suppose I had forgotten?
The exchange student from Togo
Looking primevally forlorn on the footbridge
That picture postcard afternoon
While below a boatload of girls in white shorts
Sculled masterfully along the choppy river
The coxwain barking out her commands
Or the medievalist in her greatcoat
Headed home from the library, late, nearly midnight
And vanishing
Into the forest of generators and ducts
Behind the Psych Building
Simply vanishing

Had forgotten –
In the swirling, devouring clutter
Of another year –
You, in your blue print frock at the door
Checking for your car keys

In your purse, your pockets, on the floor
When suddenly, from the stadium,
A fearsome roar –
And still not finding them
After your long, halting, indelibly sweet good-bye?

The beauty –
the way the swallows gather around the Duomo
for a few moments at dusk then scatter,
darting away across the Vale
with its checkerboard pastels dissolving into smoke
along with the hills beyond.
We saw it that one time from the Maestro's apartments,
through a little oval window above the piazza
while that awful American baritone – what's his name –
was mauling the love duet with Poppea at the end,
and she so wickedly angelic, a Veronese angel...
When de Kooning, drunk, crashed into us,
then the lot of us staggering off to that bar
overlooking the Ponte delle Torri
and finally drinking in the dawn outside Vincenzo's.
I remember the violist and cor anglais
enjoying some passion in a doorway.
Didn't they later marry? Perhaps not.
And the mezzo from Winston-Salem –
I won't tell you her name; you'll know it.
She was only a girl then, pretending
to be native, with her Neapolitan accent
and dark looks, that extravagant manner
and big laugh the divas all seem to cultivate.
But then she was only a girl, peeking
to check if her act was really coming off.
These actresses and stage performers are always a trial.
By the time you get them home
and properly unwound, the cockerels and tweety birds
already at it, they either collapse
into tears or fall dead away, shoes still on,
snoring and farting like drunken sailors.
But that night, that night it was the English poet
(now much beloved but in those days known as the *Badger*)

who was after her, her and her friend,
the pianist from Ravenna, the quieter one,
the heart-attack brunette, renowned for her Saint-Saëns.
You'll know her name too, and the recordings
she made later on with the mezzo of the Schubert lieder.
But then they were just kids, figuring it out,
suffering dainty little sips
of that tall awful yellow drink, a favorite here,
meanwhile taking the measure of it all,
as if rehearsing for a more important moment down the road.
The cunning, energy and fortitude of these creatures
almost never fails to horrify and amaze,
especially two thoroughbreds like these.
One might easily hate them for it,
but as well hate some magnificent cat in the tall grass
scanning the savannah for signs of meat.
Anyhow, the *Badger* was on form that night.
You wouldn't know him. He was young then,
really quite presentable, even appealing, I suppose,
with a shock of blond hair
and that pale distracted feral look he chose to wear.
I don't know that I've ever seen a human being drink like that.
I mean now the swollen old cunt could pass for Uncle Bertie
but in those days ... Anyhow, the *Badger*
was well along into his routine: a few bons mots,
feigned interest, the learned quote and the rest,
then his signature:
    – I don't suppose a fuck would be out of the question?
The girls took no notice, giggling between themselves
and the inevitable band of toffs and toff-y rent boys
who gather round these things. Love culture,
the toffs, can't live without it: mother's milk,
penicillin for the syphilitic.
And where would we all be without them: their dinners,
soirees, art openings, their expensive drink;
and whose appalling wives could we so generously appall?

Can't get enough of it, these toffs. Or the wives.
So this particular evening the *Badger* was right on chart,
watching, waiting, picking his spot:
    – *Ha, ha, listen, I don't suppose* . . .
when just then Signore Cor Anglais struggles to his feet,
humongous hard-on like a prow in advance of the rest,
and proceeds to blow a heavenly riff from Bruckner,
one of those alphorn bits the Bavarians so adore.
Well now, this provoked an enormous display
on the part of the toffs, sissies, remittance men,
expats – those orphans, those sorry deracinated ghosts –
the lot of them in the ruins of black tie,
shrieking like 8-year-olds at the circus
when the clown takes a flop, out of their gourds,
full up with helium, *Eeeeeeeeee* –
la vie bohème, right out there on the Corso,
a moment to be savored and regurgitated for years to come,
when the cor anglais decides to pass out,
Signora Viola all over him, beside herself,
like the final scene from – well, you name it –
the toffs, etc., carrying on like they had a ringside seat
at Krakatoa erupting on New Year's Eve;
and then I hear the mezzo – all of us,
everything else falling away, the air rippling with it –
up on her feet, singing the 'Adagiati, Poppea',
that lullaby of foreboding the nurse delivers
in Monteverdi's *L'incoronazione*, warning
of the iniquitous union ahead, but sung
with such tenderness, an unearthly sweetness.
The entire street falling silent around us,
and the *Badger* just sitting there like the rest,
hypnotized, but now his face gone slack:
astonishment? epiphany? grief? but clearly shaken
and – unimaginably out of character – about to weep.

Hyper-Berceuse: 3 a.m.

Imagine in all the debris of space
The countless trade names
    Jugurtha   *Tuolomne*   *Chert-Farms*
Some of these belong to you
Can you tell which ones
Each has its own sequence of microtones
Together they make up a kind of tune
Your tune
The ceiling and walls are star maps
Breathing, alive
Those aren't stars, darling
That's your nervous system
Nanna didn't take you to planetariums like this
Go on, touch
Lovely, isn't it
Like phosphorus on Thule Lake
Sweet summer midnights
Shimmery, like applause under the skin
Can you make it out
Almost a hiss
An old shellac LP of white noise
Playing in the distance
Foolish, troublesome boy
That hapless adventuring of yours
Be very still
Now you can hear it

Montreal

A shriek hits the membrane
that canopies the street, falls,
and the trough gets it.
Sediment thickens with it,
the dust of voices,
the smoky penumbra around streetlights,
finally settling to the ground.

A monster stirs,
under this midden we love on,
chafing himself against the crust,
too miserable to rage.

Cat jism, perfume –
the radio horn man blows
a hole through,
again blows, again with spite,
again,
until no more horn,
none.

§

Corinna in May pushed a rusty nail
deep in the soil of her sick gardenia.

All through the rain months leaf tips curled.
What buds appeared were sickly pale.
As a consumptive heroine in winter light
so fared and failed Corinna's plant.

In June, beside the burbling toilet,
a dark shellac arose in the leaves.
A bud grew fat and began to peel.
The pedicel swelled.

At last came the bloom.

Corinna of the milky thighs
unfastened her wrapper and drew a bath
so that she might wash, dream,
then wash herself again

that warm spring night in the fragrant room.

　　§

— *Get out,*

　　　　　　she said. Past
　　　　　　kindness,
unkindness,
down came no hair. Thus
ends the tale.

　　　　　　No meal of rant
　　　　　　No billy-gruff jig
　　　　　　No divots raked
　　　　　　　　from the moonlit sod

The last light lit
is the magazine shop's

with its color photos of gash
　　in baseball caps and kneesocks.

　　§

I know a pocket:
lily dust on the table,
cat in the fog.
　　　　　　It's the world turned us out
just before the whole thing blew
and virus loose
biting whatever's left to chew.

What a stroke of luck,
this isle
and only the two of us:
plenty crayfish, lots bananas
and . . .
       See over there –
It's Segovia,
Segovia playing Fernando Sor.

Epistle XIV

You ask, Aristippus, and I tell you
it's in the waiting; that the moment, like a stag,
may arrive at your doorstep as if from a cloud
and disappear before you know it,
not even the after-trace of a phantasm;
and you will have missed it for all of your scheming,
your daydreaming about lofty verses and fame,
your lunging and casting about like a spaniel
barking his way into the middle of a slough,
then unable to get out.
                              For all of your many laurels,
you wouldn't recognize it if it bit you on the ass.
You'd mistake it for some starstruck slattern
crudely making a pass. It's really hopeless, you know.
You haven't the temperament, never did.
Where you belong is in the rag trade,
wholesale, plenty of volume. There's the action,
steady, too, and regular hours:
push, and push hard enough, you've got it made.

Not like this wretched, unforgiving game,
where you can sit around for months sniffing
at the air like a patient in a convalescent ward
for mentals: knackered, reamed, a source
of amusement for all the neighbors to see.
It really is humiliating, I'm telling you.
In the end, what it comes down to is appetite –
the enforced idleness, the solitude:
nothing, hectares of nothing, litanies of nothing on microfiche.

It's simply not your line.
You're standard issue, old boy, but with claws.
If not the wholesale trade, maybe politics or law.
Trust me, Calliope, Erato – they're both twisted sisters.

Six months of Hildegard von Bingen, migraines, et al.,
next day it's Captain Cunt of the Roaring Forties,
grinding and tossing like to break your back in two.
Give it up, you old windbag. Be on your way.
The weather here stinks, and neither of these girls is for you.

Christmastime in Coronado

The attack jets come in low
over the ocean
past the tennis courts and the Duchess's cottage,
in tandem
low over the Navy golf course
headed for the North Island airstrip
then wheel to the left
out over the water again,
the afternoon's last light
making a movie set of the offshore islands
around and back once more
past the grand old wooden hotel and its cupolas
with a series of watery, high-pitched *whups*
and disappear over the ridge.

The town seems very still, almost empty, rich.
Christmas displays in store windows.
A goodly stream of cars.
The traffic lights make a sound too, bird-like.
I often get confused.
The roaring overhead. The traffic noise.
There is no place to go.

Out on the Silver Strand
the joggers and sweethearts take in the sunset
the air overhead as busy as war
Skyhawks, Vigilantes, Intruders
the cargo and surveillance planes
sub hunters, gunships
Phantom, Tomcat, Cobra...
It must have given the late President
great succor out there in his compound
those long troubled evenings in San Clemente
to see the lights

and track the arc of the distant thunder
as he sat, with a drink, looking
out that enormous window at the sea, the stars
a blur of light from the distant pier.

I have read, of the late President
from those who had been close to him, through it all
that he had in him a reflective
one might even say philosophical cast of mind.
I wouldn't know to say it wasn't true.
I wouldn't know to say.
But I myself have been thinking constantly of America.
Only of late, only here
with the might of the nation roaring overhead
around the clock
spewing vapor from their strakes
going fucking nowhere
and noisily coming back.

[1998]

A History of Western Music

April of that year in the one country
was unusually clear
and with *brisk* northeasterlies
'straight from the Urals'.
Their ancient regent at long last succumbed
and laid to rest after much ceremony.
Sinatra was everywhere that spring,
in the hotel lobbies, toilets, shops –
'Fly Me to the Moon', 'You Make Me Feel
So Young', name it.
On TV a computer-generated Weimaraner
sang 'I Did It My Way'
in a gravelly barroom baritone.
                              – He only weighed 130 lbs.,
Ava Gardner was to have remarked,
soaking wet,
but a hundred of those lbs. was cock.

Whereas, the season before
in the other country to the west
no matter into which room you walked
it would have been the *heart-wrenching adagietto*
from Mahler's *Symphony No. 5.*
Only a small country,
it had endured a long, *famously tragic* history.
Still, it was more than passing strange,
not halfway through your plate of mussels,
the tremblingly _____ adagietto,
showering you with the debris
of Gustav Mahler's *tortured* soul, True,
wife Alma was a troublesome slut;
we know this of her and choose to forgive.
But what of this late Romantic excess,

this anthem of the Hapsburg twilight,
in a cruelly served and windswept land?

We had only lately come over the Sally Gap
across the bogland, down through the glen,
and were walking slowly
along the Lower Lake of Glendalough.
Afternoon had turned toward evening,
and with it came a chill.
And with the chill a mist
had begun to gather over the lake.
– *This is a haunted place*, I heard her say.

It was quiet then. We were the last ones there.
Only a patch of birdsong. Only the wind.
Unheeded, from somewhere *out of the blue*,
– *Liberace*, she said, and nothing more.
We continued on our walk and listened,
if just to the silence.
This would have been an hour St Kevin knew
and savored
before retreating to the Gatehouse
and into the monastery for evening prayer.
One can imagine a stillness forming around him there
like those halos of gold or ocher
that surround the sacred figures in frescoes.

Much as they do with 'Lee'
in one of his brocaded lamé jumpsuits
with its sequins catching the spotlights,
enorbing the performer in brilliant rays
as he smiles *coquettishly* to the Vegas crowd
then turns to deliver the first
in a series of *thunderous* glissandos,
somehow finding his way back
to a climactic, *magnificently rousing* chorus

of that million seller
and *timeless classic*,
                    'Moon River'.

Sleeping Dog

The terrier will not relinquish
his hold on it,
frozen in attack he clenches stillness
and would shake it like a rat
but for its vastness.

Bad William trembles,
electrons crackling in his wisp
of beard, warrior-sage,
while all of the Heavens' soldiers
swoop down in staggered assault:
Canis, Ursus, Aries,
first one then the next.

Willie, jump.
No, there, there, Willie, in the rushes.
A terrible exchange.
Stout Willie.
Willie the Brave.
Your back, Willie.
Willie, five o'clock high.

Behold, your fearsome arsenal,
its plenitude of feints,
its murderous sorties.
Fair William,
Willie the True,
now is your moment arrived:

Sweetie boy,
you lovely little killer-toy
Willie, hold on.

The Visit

She was wearing a beard,
which, of itself, did not seem odd
nor in any way
diminished my longing.

It was a fine full beard
grizzled in places,
and rather nicely answered
the sweep of her hair,

which was as I remembered.
She was 19, still,
and spoke terribly fast.
I hurried after her remarks,

so delicious and filled
with wit, invention:
a launderer's shop, a taxi's bray,
became a revelation.

How she'd flourished in New York.
I knew she would.
After each fresh burst of talk
I made her say again

the last few words or phrase
so as not to lose a thing.
How I adored her, still,
and treasured these visits,

her incarnations too,
always herself, but different,
my heart rushing out to her,
my adored.

And always slipping away,
in a crowd, on a platform –
like grasping at shadows,
always the same.

This time a hotel room,
littered, filthy,
the owner tromping through,
my finger cut badly,

spotting the carpet with blood
as I tear around
looking for a phone book, an address,
I am not clear,

except that we are done.
I know that well.
I know that deep.
But not her ways, or when she'll come.

Pulp 'n' Gumbo Sonnet

NOWHERE PRUNE TOWN MORPHS INTO HIGH-TECH EDEN

FAT RAPIST RE-JAILED

BURGLARS TAKE GUILLOTINE AND HITLER'S PIANO

DISNEY HIRES KISSINGER

SHARK TAKES GROOM AS WIFE ESCAPES

PRISON SEX VIDEO STARS DEAD SICKO

RUNAWAY OSTRICH PANICS LAS VEGAS

SGT BILKO MISTAKEN FOR DALAI LAMA

STRANGE TRIUMPHS IN SUDDEN DEATH

TSUNAMI'S CORPSE LAGOON

SQUARCIALUPI STANDS UP FOR DWARFS

FRESH NABOKOV STOPS PREDATORS

NO REGGAE IN TAIPAN

I WARNED THEM IT WAS A MISTAKE TO INVITE OLIVER

A History of Western Music: Chapter 4

The reader may know of the Jesuit Father Lewis Bernard Castel (1688–1757), renowned for his 'clavecin pour les yeux' and his discoveries in 'l'art peinture le son', the art of painting sound. What could be so ingenious as to render sound visible and make the eyes confident of all the pleasures that music can bring to the ears? Music has always, throughout time, found comparison with color, but it was the German Kircher, a man with a geometrical mind, who first deduced that what was perceptible to the ears might also be made perceptible to the eyes. Of this phenomenon, as it relates to music, he called 'the monkey of light'.

Father Castel, much taken by this notion of the *simian lucis*, began in earnest his work on the 'ocular harpsichord', and twenty years later, on the 21st of December, 1755, the day of Saint Thomas, patron saint of the Incredulous and Harpsichords, this learned Jesuit, who had out an invitation to fifty persons of rank, some from abroad, lighted not less than one hundred candles.

Putting behind him the skeptics and detractors (I tremble here to recite the names of Messieurs Buffon and De Mairan), the Father demonstrated, in a mere half hour of playing, the marvel of his creation: that when C is heard, blue will be seen; when red is seen, E will be heard. And that the *chiaroscuro* will answer to the *grave* D, while the color orange takes up the interval between E and F, etc. In his achievement, Father Castel succeeded in doubling music, so that the deaf may see and the blind may hear, and those with their sensibilities entire may enjoy music in its fullest measure.

Well, the result was much commented upon at the time, this remarkable instrument of the Father Castel. But there were those, outside the cirles that matter, where the ladies carry bouquets so that the perfume might mingle happily with the powder on their hair, and one in particular, a certain Migrenne, who were not content with the Father's 'pretty divagations' and sought to bring braver purpose to his invention.

Of this Migrenne, I shall not say too much. He was known to be a Freemason, even a friend of Mozart. As to the rest, the details are hidden from us, except to say that this Migrenne heard colors; that is, a certain chord might appear to him a yellowish orange, and when played an octave higher, turn almost white, but with overtones of pale green and violet. It was Migrenne's ambition to sit down at his instrument and illuminate the entire map of the world, including all of its Perus, Japonias and Archipelagos.

Have you seen the machines people carry about in the streets that show *curiosities* and *rarities* through a glass? By pulling little strings, scenes of Cities, Castles, Wars and everything you wish for may be brought before your eyes. Migrenne, by moving his fingers along the keyboard, with its sharps made of ebony and naturals of bone, like a god, would set out to play the world into being, coloring it as his imaginings prompted, almost dreaming it into being, note by note.

On the inside lid of any good French harpsichord it is usual to find a painting: Cupid and Psyche, Castor and Pollux, perhaps chinoiserie: Chinamen smoking and fiddling in a garden, that sort of thing. Orpheus charming the beasts: this is an especially popular motif. Migrenne, with his timbres, dusty, moist or lute-like, tart as a green apple or chocolaty, would paint over the gods and goddesses, the putti, castles and bergerie, and bring forth in their place his Africas, his

Capes and Plateaus. And by applying certain pedal tones on the instrument, making a sarabande move dolefully, or by appoggiatura, a certain chromaticism or an especially brisk toccata, our friend Migrenne would temper or modulate as he went.

Clouds he would color myrrh, sometimes crimson, or for variety an agate or *pigeon neck*. Smoke, sails, and flags were always blue bice, and castles red-lead. Of trees, some he made grass green, others burnt umber, Rome was pale rose and ocher. Tiles he colored vermilion, spires and pinnacles blue. The seashore and lakes were indigo. Ships amber, Spain saffron, but in places a thin wash of brown. Most principal towns and cities were carmine, the hills surrounding gamboge. Brazil was pink and blue and red, like parrots. Meadows straw color. The sea a pale celadon.

You know the story of Daphne and the laurel tree. These were living maps Migrenne brought into creation, wet and breathing: the Burgundian Ambience entire, the roofs of Antwerp a copper green. In sequence of note and phrasing he played islets and downs, gold-topped basilicas, the sea boiling away at the edge of the Moluccas.

Music is fugitive, living a moment and leaving nothing behind. So it was these maps of Migrenne would pass by quickly before one's eyes, only to disappear without a trace. As to their verisimilitude and utility, one surely would be able to find his way among the cities, shrines and entrepôts, and through the wilderness between. But these maps had little to do with exactness of latitude. Rather, the estimable Migrenne put a prism over this world, in order to color it with his playing, visiting any one place only so long as the reverberation of a single plucked string.

The Installation

Until it all turned into a waxworks
The lot of them
In the same old rooms
Same lamps, chairs, wainscoting
The piano still there, out of tune
Sheet music under the seat

A period tableau, late '50s
But off, somehow, dark
A hint of menace in the shadows
It could almost be something out of Kienholz
But eastern, domestic
Taped voices issuing from hidden speakers

How strange to be in the midst of it
After so long
In a kind of museum, among strangers
Indifferent, perhaps amused
Making comments about physiognomies
Or the upholstery

Indulging their surmise about character
Intimate appraisals
From the recorded bits of conversation
Played over and over again
Recycled every few minutes

How freakishly accurate
Not a few manage to be, while others
Others find nothing at all
Or manage only to be foolish
Or unkind

Do they recognize us
I wonder
It is an agony to be here
Terrible, one can hardly breathe
But so frozen in wonderment
That even with the rest of them pushing
Trying to get close
It is impossible to leave

Lavinia, si placet

Enough, enough then, Lavinia, stop.
They were nearly children themselves at your start,
neither rich, attractive nor terribly smart.
Now, what small fame and money you've got
has been purchased at the expense of those very same two

who nursed, kept and soothed you, dandled
and sang to you, and now keep your latest volume
and press clippings close by to show friends
what their own little Lavinia has come to.
Sure, it all went bad fast after you hit 12

but, truth is, you were never a bargain.
It only follows you're a hideous adult.
Your incessant whining about Mommy's hard heart
and Daddy's vile...
God, I can't bear to trot it all out –

has fetched you prize after prize, sinecures
on charming old campuses with trellises and shrubs.
But worse, worse still, you've gone and turned on Mark,
just like the parents you exhausted once,
then, as a subject, exhausted again.

Yes, Mark, who kissed and indulged you, opened his heart,
only to have you pick up your pen and write
about his belligerent penis...
Lavinia, I beseech you, when will it all stop?
Your renown at this metastasizes unchecked

as you devour everyone, anyone, near to you,
nourishing yourself then passing the rest.

The Single Gentleman's Chow Mein

The ants are very bad tonight
and the poison is old.
It's the rains that bring them out,
you know. The first big storm
and there they are,
all over the counter with their scouts
in advance, under the sink mat
and mason jars, probing
the way they do.

They have a smell, of that I'm certain,
a formic aroma,
that gathers round them in the heat
of their frenzy; I don't know
but that they take it on outside
and bring it along with them
on their journey through these walls.

But they do enjoy it, the bait.
It must still have some strength.
See how they cluster.
You need only stir the paste
with the end of a match
and the arsenic's perfume blooms again.
They really do love it.
Watch how they feed.
Soon they will take the poison back
from where they have come,
back to their nest,
and destroy their queen.

I only ordered half a pound this time.
Most evenings – yes, most –
I would probably get a whole and leave some

for lunch next day,
perhaps a casserole.
But just tonight it was looking,
well, a trifle sad,
sitting there in its steam tray
for half an eternity.

You know how it tends to get slow
after the lunch trade.
The one batch in its grease for hours,
taking on that viscous, cloudy look,
almost jaundice under the fluorescent lights.
From time to time the homeless wander in
and bargain for some rice,
perhaps a spear of wilted broccoli.
And if it's quiet, the Lotus will oblige.

But I do like it.
I add things on, you see:
vegetables, all manner of condiments
and treats, a shrimp
or scallop, or two, or three.
It's very nice the way I do it,
and never the same way twice.

They know me down there,
at the Lotus, I mean,
and have done for years.
The girls behind the counter change.
– *Ah, ha, chow mein,*
they say, smiling, when they know me.
It's quite nice, really.
One of them, oh, three years back
was a stunner, terribly pretty;
taking a night course, as I recall.
– *You look like professor, no?*

she said to me one day, a trifle severe
in delivery but very sweet.
I've never been with a Chinese.

The large black man is dancing
He is dancing in his head
On the stage of the Salle Pleyel
And the Parisians are watching
As he takes one step to the left
But, look, his foot is not touching
The ground, as if it's too hot
Or cold, or not to be found there at all
Then slamming it down
And spinning around
Like a drunk in his funny hat

The large black man is dancing
On the stage of the Salle Pleyel
He has gotten up from the piano
And begun his silly dance
Lurching, first one way, then...
Wait, he is changing his mind
Frozen there in space, on just one leg
His drummer and bass, Pierre,
That is, and Claude, puzzling through
What he has left behind
Soldiering on, regardless
Wondering where they misplaced the time
On the stage of the Salle Pleyel

The large black man is dancing
Dancing in his head
On the stage of the Salle Pleyel
And hundreds of French are watching him
Twitch or swat
Away an imaginary chord in order to make room
For the next, with a pirouette
Courtly as a maitre d' on roller skates

The large black man, the large
Black man is dancing
And the Parisians are watching
Nervously. But the drummer, Pierre
That is, and Claude on bass
Are beginning to get it
They are watching the black man's dance
And think they've found it
Relax, *mes chers*
We are nearing the end of the tune

The black, black man is dancing
Dancing in his head
On the stage of the grand *théâtre*
And the lovers of jazz are there
They are out there in force
Watching the black man from America
Watching the black man dance
It is 1954
And the tune is 'Trinkle, Trinkle'
What are they to do
What to make
Of the black man up there dancing
Is he *fou*
Does he not know where he is or who
Is in the audience watching
There is the editor of *Jazz Hot*
Section C, Aisle 12, Seat # 2
He will be confused, no
Is he being made the fool
What are they all to do

Pierre and Claude, the drummer,
That is, and the contrabass
They think, OK, I've got it
Where the accents drop

Where not
And those very weird spaces between
(*Ha*, *ha*, *ha*, but not really)

The large black man
In his coat and his tie
And the funny little hat
And crazy grin
The large black man is
Dancing

Citronella and Yellow Wasps

Before the heat and after
The little pink beeper shop and the flamingo
In the logo
Same color as the icing on the cookies inside
And the votive candles that heal bad sprains
Also, the billboards overhead
Through the dusty branches
Big square decals mounted against sky
A bit of nose here, some lettering
Jesus or barbecue
Exit 205
Cobalt blue background cut out of sky
'Clouds with Hanging Panels'
When the light is right at that place it finds
For 20 minutes or so
Only that
So many fugitive spaces
– *You give us 22 minutes and we'll give you the world*
I could even tell you which film to use
If I had a moment
Soundtrack by . . .
Theremin, slide guitar and aeoliphone
Messiaen and Blind Boy Fuller
The truth pours north
I meant trucks
Maquiladora   sisal   tin
Box girders and columns
Concrete cantilevers overhead flowing
All the way to Minneapolis
Heroin and mangoes
Everything in the grass beginning to wake
And bite

It's so dry
A fine mist of particulates
Settling in
Feed dust   nickel   sulfates
Sound travels funny in the heat
Blaise, Blaise
Dare I ever forget you
Tequila and sandals
Methamphetamine
Humping it all the way to Brownsville
Hook 'em, Horns
NASCAR   Talk radio
Crank it, Hurley, crank it
All the way through Mosquitoville
The whole long stretch to Mesa Junction
Wild light
A rattle by the storm drain
Red Rooster
Speed kills
No lie the way these people paint
Things so bright

An Englishman Abroad

FOR CHRISTOPHER LOGUE

The talk-radio host is trying to shake the wacko
with only a minute left
to get in the finance and boner-pill spots
before signing off,
the morning news team already at the door
and dairy vans streaming
from the gates of WholesomeBest, fanning out
across the vast plateau.
Fair skies, high cumulus cloud –
the birds are in full throat as dawn ignites
in the east, rinsing the heavens with a coral pink.

What power and wealth,
the foreign visitor reflects from his bed
in the quaint, *old west* hotel,
two military jets thundering by overhead.
He takes in the embroidered homilies on the walls,
the highboy and phony Windsor chairs,
and begins to smell the coffee and bacon
frying down the stairs. He is not at all ready
to say good-bye
to this resourceful, generous, open-faced tribe
with its matchless plumbing and inexhaustible vistas.

To the west, prevailing winds
deposit a vapor of phenols, benzene, sulfides
across the grasslands, choking back
the cinquefoil and flowering tansy,
slowly dismantling the proteins in the curlew's bill.
He remembers the pretty blond attendant
at the laundrette, her shy but persistent
queries about his accent and native Portsmouth,

and that lingering smile.
Angel food cake   black camisole
         Voucheron   spike heels:
revery, tumescence, gladness – When just then

the clock radio comes on
with its farm report followed by an ancient Procol Harum tune
that takes him uncomfortably back, way back
to a calamitous party in Shepherd's Bush.
What a hateful dismal shitty little village
London really is.
Should he have pursued her? In earnest?
She seemed keen enough at the time
but these amorous gambits of late
have one after another come a cropper.
One tires of being made to feel the fool.

They gave him everything, these good people.
A magnificent stage, first-rate lighting
and packed houses every night.
They'd have wept real tears on the West End to see it.
And *here*, in the middle of blinking nowhere.
Just look at the color of those clouds.
Rosy-fingered dawn, my ass.
This show's in Technicolor.
The telephone. Must be his minder.
– *Yes, yes, I'll be ready downstairs at 8.*
Excellent girl. I should remember
to send her a little something when I get back.
Toffee or some silly English thing or other.

They can't get enough of all that, poor dears.
What was that joke the department Chair told?
No matter. A most amusing chap.
You don't suppose it will be another of those
awful little commuter jets?

[45]

I'll be shattered by the time I get to Denver,
much less Heathrow.
What was that darling girl's name?
Jeanie. Janie. Joanie. Jeanine. *Jeanette.*
Yes, that was it. Lovely creature.
Why do I scruple so?
It's an affliction, that's what it is.
Bloody hell . . .

'Lil' Bits: American Foundlings

(*Las Vegas*)

TERRIBLE'S LUBE
SERENUS HYPNOSIS

(*Chinatown*)

TUNE GET
COIN & BULLION

(*Rock and Roll*)

JUNE & THE EXIT WOUNDS

(*Las Vegas*, II)

SHRIMP COCKTAIL SPORTS & CELEBRITIES

(*War Stories*)

... THEN THE FRIGGIN' DE-IONIZER CAUGHT FIRE

(*Japantown*)

GOLD TEETH — MR BLING BLING

(*Flora*)

HEART'S EASE
KISS-HER-THE-BUTTERY

(Rock and Roll, II)

CANDY BUTCHERS

(Las Vegas, III)

VASECTOMY REVERSAL
METAL KINGS

(Free Advice)

ROOT HOG OR LOSE YOUR ACORN

After Lady Murakami

These sleeping used car dealerships
and blowing wrappers

how many lost evenings
the meagerness, the waste

when suddenly the squeals
of a transvestite

about to gobble her cell phone

§

Just as I found myself
in the dentist chair

only yesterday
hands clenched against my thighs

so I find myself here
in this seat

heart in my throat

as you walk into the room

§

The cherry blossoms are late
this year

I had nearly forgotten about them.

the pleasure they bring
always fresh, a delicacy to it

because the poets say so

or just because
§

I had on my favorite kimono
not the most precious

but the one that calls attention
to my eyes

yet when you turned
it was as if a thought, like a tick

had started to bite
and then changed its mind
§

Do they know who I am
these gibbering little foreigners

coarse, frenzied
like perfumed monkeys

her servant's averted eyes
dew on her sleeve and all the rest

none of it, never even heard
of Lady Murakami

as they crowd me aside
at the sale bin

A History of Western Music: Chapter 26

FOR BETSY JOLAS

... chestnuts in blossom, you know,
the Sarah Vaughan version where Clifford Brown
comes in halfway through
like the Sun King into a rumpled, smoky bedroom...

In the hotel elevator
with its worn plush and elaborate fittings
a Tadd Dameron large band arrangement
circa 1950-something
comes out of the overhead speaker
as if poured through history's electrified sieve.

The art of the *American Negro Jazz Musician*
is much beloved here
among this enlightened and tolerant race
with their stylized, bird-like gestures
and agile little faces.
                    – *Hello,*
says the black man with the trumpet
to the chestnut vendor, circa 1950-something,
receiving a wave and hearty greeting.

Outside, along the boulevards,
stanchions and chestnuts surpliced with posters,
it is election time:
                    M. Bontemps Roulé vs The Major,
both villains,
both, too, acquainted with a certain Nathalie,
dark and playful Nathalie,
four flights up, second door on the left.
She has a favorite tape, this one,
some lightly throbbing *Chaâbi*

along with a brooding jazz film score
circa ...

Operas, revolutions, outrages at the Salon –
c'est complet.
                A small new museum
will open near the *Quay American Negro Jazz Musician*,
with photos of the many visiting greats –
Dameron, Brown, et al. –
posing with their arms around the chestnut vendor
and a darkly pretty girl, a favorite
among the musicians, a certain Nathalie.

They are all waving heroically
that gray chilly afternoon by the river,
like something out of a Géricault.
No, make that Doisneau.

They are waving at the photographer,
probably to a small crowd of fans,
and, unwittingly, even to us,
who stare back at them impassively
from behind our screens.

Back

How familiar it all slowly becomes:
a photograph
still murky in its chemical bath;
a tune or aroma
not quite placed but close in the mind,
and then, *yes, ah, that, my my* . . .

The pastels and hills, the addled geometry –
desolation
perched on the gut like a seagull on a piling.
An outpost, by the sea,
so very far from anything and its back turned.
In defiance? Hardly,
nothing so emphatic in this cool, silvered air.
Bewilderment, perhaps.
A studied casualness. Yes. That.

And if a woman,
beautiful, surely, at the very least,
distant, vain. But foolishly so,
endearingly.
Spaghetti straps and the rest.
And vague.
Ceremonially so. Stupid maybe.
Blinkered, of course.
But handsomely turned out and well-practiced
in so very many of the comforts
that slipping away from her atmosphere
involves real pain.

One finds one's way,
slowly;
as there is no place to really hurry, is there?
Always in the small things:

a box of staples in the sideboard's drawer,
or the garlic press,
found at last behind the vinegars and pastes.
Who would have left it there?
So many people have passed through in my absence.

I have been away a long time,
forgotten just how quiet it can seem.
No Penelope, no good blind Argos chivied by fleas.
No suitors to slay.
How terribly long it takes:
the books and closets and outside plants
finding their ways back into one's head,
where and in what order.
Away for so long I'm other than I was,
having again to learn simply how to be here,
as if having another go at the piano
after how many years.

Balling at 50

You are lovely and I am not,
But glad
      Of Nature's Grace
That we Two should Together make
      Full Chimp, Toto's Lair,
      Jallalaphontina's Caper

      In this the Total World
With its Rhumb Lines of Electron Spoor
         Above the Steeples
      And Limewash and Courses
           Of Brick
        Spalled or Repointed

        Thronged Escalators
        Great Vats of Honey

        Remind, pray, tell
How thus the Streaming Familiar
        Is made to transfigure
Magick'd in the Candle's Glow
        From Meat to Spirit
        And back once more
        With Singing Jolts
          And good Result
        Sans undo Care
          Such Swyvving rare
        This grand Plaisance
         In Dalliance
So strong, so strange, so well
        Fair star, do tell

Epistle VIII

It's simply untrue, Maecenas, that I do not care for nature.
A vile canard: I do, but not unadorned. I need architecture,
    streets,
and, not least, the human form, to frame, contrast and
    ornament.
A birch among a sea of birches does not enchant.
Rather, give me a birch, say, over there in the moonlight,
to the left of the belvedere, by itself or part of a small stand,
with ample space around it to show off its charms to
    advantage.
Hey, now, spare me the *decadent* and *jaded* bit, old dear.
You like your little Claudia's tits and ass all the better
when they're showcased and partially hid by those ribbons of
    silk.

You see that storm headed our way from the southwest,
those dark clouds blowing in at an angle like an advance
    guard,
racing across the sky above the Medical Center?
One needs those featureless blocks up there, I tell you,
to provide us with the theater, the spectacle of it.
A front coming in over any old hill is no big deal,
only another patch of rotten weather.
But check out the values there, in the charcoal-bellied,
    mottled clouds
and how they blend or stand against the pale stone of the
    towers,
or how that stone fares in the storm's particular light.
There's more art in that than your insipid vineyards,
being driven half mad by blackflies, dodging rattlers.

Just watch how the eucalyptus twist and writhe in the wind,
tossing their crowns and branches like the dancers we saw –
    when was it? –

the other night. Nature takes its metaphors from city life,
and the other way round, each diminished when left to its
    own devices.
But of the two, it's town, I say, proves better for poetic figures,
not least because nature is to be found in any city you look,
if only a pitiful avocado plant on a shelf somewhere,
dragging its rhizomes in a highball glass. Nature is always
    there,
indoors and out: a cat, a pigeon, a phthisic sweet gum,
not to mention the sky. A city has its very own weather,
altogether different from the nearby countryside.
And a moon is never so pretty as in a poisoned sky.
Besides, every city has a park, its own public greensward
with flowers and trees. How much of that does one really
    need?

There's good reason why the folks you find up-country tend
    to be dull.
It's because they spend their days talking to animals, you
    know.
Listen, don't get me wrong, I think all those songbirds are
    great:
the waxwing's trill and rattle, the warbler's hoarse little
    chuif.
Perfectly delicate, marvelous stuff, an overture to cocktails.
But the birdsong for me, right up there with Bartók and
    Monk,
is never straight up but part of a mix – footsteps, traffic,
fountains, shouts – that beggar Cage or Stockhausen.
Accident, contingency: it's *city* nature, Maecenas, that's for
    me,
not those endless manured fields, lowing cattle and whatever
    sheep do.
I'd like to once walk through those hills you go on about
without getting shit all over my shoes. You leave that part
    out.

Frankly, I'm nauseated by these bucolic rhapsodies
you and your kind indulge yourselves with and the public
    eats up.
Exactly who do you think you're fooling? You're city boys,
one and all, and with your apartments still in town, as well,
so you can slip back in for a secret shag and proper meal
    after.
You're in town, Maecenas, more than you will comfortably
    admit.
C'mon, babe, it's me, Augie-boy, friends since we were kids.
But hey, I'm not unamused at the rustic posture you affect,
the mud-splattered wellingtons, the coarse fabric of your
    pants.
Your conversation, the pleasures of your table, remain a
    delight,
at least so long as I can make it back to town that same night.
But please, I'm begging, Maecenas, show an old friend some
    respect:
spare me the update on feed prices, these lectures on the good
    life.

On Waking in a Room and Not Knowing
Where One Is

There is a bureau and there is a wall
and no one is beside you.
Beyond the curtains only silence,
broken now and again by a car or truck.
And if you are very still
an occasional drip from the faucet.
Such are the room's acoustics
it is difficult to place exactly where from.
Also, the tick of the clock.
It is very dark.
There exist all manner of blacks,
lampblack, for instance,
much favored by the ancients,
so deep and dense
and free of any shades of gray
or brown. But this,
this dark is of another order,
compounded of innumerable shadows,
a weave of them.
One is able to make out shapes.
It is not restful, to be like this, here,
nor is it a fearful place.
In a moment or two you will know
exactly where you are,
on which side the door,
your wallet, your shoes,
and what today you'll have to do.

Cities each have a kind of light,
a color even,
or set of undertones
determined by the river or hills
as well as by the stone

of their countless buildings.
I cannot yet recall what city this is I'm in.
It must be close to dawn.

The Tunnel of Love

In a place of trampled peanuts,
like Hansel and Gretel at the end of their spoor,
we come at last to our journey's end.

Dusk brings on the lights
and one can hear, if only faintly, music and screams
from deep inside.
                Leg-weary, only half-awake,
stunned by the game-booths, barkers and speed,

the time has come,
we have finally arrived
for what you and I knew all along
would be the day's last ride.

But first, a lemonade with ice
to startle the hot brain and sweeten the tongue.
Our prow slams through the door
and we are in night.
                – *Darling, darling*, she whispers,
tell me what you'd truly like.
                – *Tickle my nose, if you would,*
I ask her.
        Aatchoo
          Gesundheit

How happy we are with the gimcrack horrors,
the cackles and groans,
alone,
      moving slowly.

Having exhausted the musical offerings of Antwerp,
that ruin of a once great port,
with the *parlous* condition of its organs
and detestably out of tune *serpent*,
sounding like an *Essex calf* in anger,

Burney continued up the Rhine,
bumping along miserably in his post chaise,
complaining as he went: from Aachen to Cologne,
Darmstadt to Mannheim, its Elector
away for the summer with his orchestra in Schwetzingen.
Upon hearing a local fife and drums:
– *There had been no occasion to quit London.*

The incessant chimes and carillons behind him,
Burney crossed the *terrible* range of Wetteravia,
finally reaching Frankfurt, more exhausted
even than he had been after crossing Mount Cenis,
to find the steeple in the hands of the Lutherans,
and the women unspeakably ugly.
Not to mention the *insolent* postmaster,
sullen postilions, customs tariffs, and *villainous* roads.

Only to arrive, at last, in Schwetzingen,
its orangery grander than even Versailles's,
where he would hear the famous Stamitz perform
and the celebrated orchestra afforded
ample room and verge enough
for all of its *powers* and *delicate beauties.*
Here, with Cannabich conducting,
where the court in three things excelled:
in its *military*, its *music* and its *hunt*;

the orchestra that gave us *crescendo* and *diminuendo*,
the greatest of its age,
even young Mozart himself agog at their musicianship,
writing delirious notes home to Poppa;
Burney, Dr Charles Burney,
author of the learned *General History of Music*,
a work appearing in four volumes,
and delivering unto the author great renown,
would find that summer's afternoon in Schwetzingen

a *want of truth* in the oboes
and a displeasing *sharpness* among the bassoons.

The Art Farm

Another season comes to a close.
Sunflowers nod, the mallards grow restive
and hoarfrost sparkles on the lawns
well into morning. After some discussion,
the badminton nets finally come down.
For one last time the cleaning ladies
strip off the bedclothes of the week's guest artist
and do what they can with the wine stains.
– *Jerk*, they say to themselves, village girls
with almost no experience of art.

Like a caravan, the Toyotas, Saabs and 4 x 4s
head south, breaking up among the interchanges
north of Boston and heading their separate ways:
some to the nation's colleges,
where they take up their residencies once more,
even with the thunder of football season upon them;
some to the warrens and fastnesses of Brooklyn,
where the young, these days, position themselves.

Behind them, a cold front from Canada moves in
across the wooded peaks and ridges, settling
among the many valleys and turning to mush
the late vegetables, finishing off
what's left of the blackberries, deep in their brambles.
Beauty is difficult. Yes, yes, of course it is.
How would it be otherwise? Of course, of course.
But what a lot of good talk about process

and stimulating tête-à-têtes. Energized, inspired, even,
one leaves this peaceful place. *Fructified*:
yes, that would be the word, exactly.
Reluctantly, one returns to the world
and all its quotidian bother, fructified.

And with them goes their art, these cheerful
and satisfied customers, packed safely away
in their trunks and back seats: the rolled canvases
and tools; manuscripts-in-progress
safely transferred to hard disk and awaiting

application of all that encouragement and sound counsel:
ready for that final, determined drive
to completion and a great big FUCK YOU for you know who.
Dwayne closes up the place for winter, stapling
plastic up over the bookshelves, the Ping-Pong table,
bringing in the deck chairs and the rest.
Good ol' Dwayne. The traffic begins to congeal,
just east of Hartford and the turnoff near Poughkeepsie.
It doesn't really matter, does it?
You're going to hit it sooner or later.
Sooner or later, it can't be helped.

Christmas in Chinatown

They're off doing what they do
and it is pleasant to be here without them
taking up so much room.
They are safely among their own,
in front of their piles of meat, arguing
about cars and their generals,
and, of course, with the TV going all the while.

One reads that the digestive wind passed by cattle
is many times more destructive to the atmosphere
then all of the aerosol cans combined.
How does one measure such a thing?
The world has been coming to an end
for 5,000 years. If not tomorrow,
surely, one day very soon.

R_x *for S*

Nap. Go looking for the fox
in Holland Park at dusk. And if you see him,
and he sees you, well then.
Smoke even more ganj, and at hours
you're unaccustomed. Nothing
must be allowed to interfere
with this, your willed indolence.
Set forth among your dreams as a traveler
in a distant rain forest, awonder
at the hibiscus-like carnivorous blooms
spangling the tendrils and moss.
They nor the sleek ebony *jrdaka*
will bite, nor even give affront
because you are swaddled in a cloud,
a molecular raiment of scent
by which they will know you.
The world is full, full of care,
grief but another tortured littoral,
hostage to the sea and rough weather.
Decamp to the sheltered valleys.
You will find comfort there, and safety,
and, for no reason, remember a colored plate
belonging to a favored storybook
your father would read to you
when you were only a very small girl.
Sleep.

The Bus Barn at Night

Motion is not a condition
but a desire
to be outside of one's Self
and all desire must be swept away

so saith fatso Gautama
bus-like
under the shade of some shrub
in the Deer Park
in some grove
some municipal greensward
chewing a leaf
that has left him stoned
as a stone
stone-like
mouthing this sententious drivel
some errand boy
some rich man's son
dutifully sets down
on a dusty tablet
ignoring the insects and snakes

After midnight
under the arc lights
like a giant soundstage
the abandoned set
of an action spectacular
Mrs Kiniski's team
goes bus to bus
hoovering candy wrappers
crumbs
and then with their scrapers
attending to the grease
and impacted filth

and gum
as Rudolfo sluices away
in the southeast corner
and the boss, with a sigh
comes to the end
of Herman Hesse's *Siddhartha*

Phalanx upon phalanx
of impassive Buddha-wagons
silver hulls and red trim
Fleet of the Three Jewels
the Attainment & Perfection
City Transit Corp.
hosed down, lubricated and tuned
in the Eternity Shop
the Cave of Illumination and Fumes

Soda Water with a Boyhood Friend

He is in the canals behind your forehead,
paddling,
        or in the high, vaulted rooms
your speech rays round itself,
still and alert as a hunter in the blind,
taking measure if that, yes, it really is you,
against what he has down
                  in the log of his remembering

over a cigar and club soda. Ah,
the good bogs and rushes,
the forest beyond with its tweet tweet   tweet,
cranked to a blur, a hum,
a time-lapse cavalcade of scene
fade scene *dissolve* scene spilling across the wraparound
screen and soaked in by the multitudes,
                multitudes of kindled selves.

The Hereafter

At the gates to the Hereafter,
a rather drab affair, might as well be a union hall
in south Milwaukee, but with shackled
sweating bodies along the walls,
female, chiefly, and not at all miserable,
straining like bored sultanas at their fetters,
each of them singing a separate song.
A Semitic chap – the greeter, I suppose –
gives me the quick once-over
and most amused he seems to be. Has me figured.
Not unlike a gent I met only last week,
a salesman at a stereo shop on Broadway.
So, he says. Nothing more,
Sew buttons, says I, in a cavalier mood
and why not.
                    Ushers me into a tiny cinema,
a two-seater, really quite deluxe,
a great big Diet Coke in the cupholder,
fizzing away.
                    – *OK?* he asks.
I nod and the film unrolls.
A 20-million-dollar home movie it is,
featuring yours truly: at the foot
of the stairs with the dog, mounting
Josette in a New Smyrna love nest,
a fraught kitchen showdown with Mom,
the suicide, car wreck, home run.
You know what these things are like:
the outlandish hairdos, pastel bathroom fixtures.
The editing is out of this world,
the whole shebang in under an hour:
the air-raid drill on Wednesday morning,
1957, when Tito wet his pants;
there I am, beside myself with laughter,

miserable little creature.
The elemental, slow-motion machinery
of character's forcing house.
Even with all the fancy camera angles,
jump cuts and the rest,
might as well be a chain of short features:
Animal Husbandry, Sexual Hygiene,
Lisboa by Night...
What a lot of erections, voidings, pretzels,
bouncing the ball against the stoop.
She really did love you, all along.
These jealousies and rages of yours,
like a disgusting skin condition
that never entirely goes away.
You, you...
What catalogs of failure, self-deception...

And then the lights come back on,
likewise the choir's splintered polyphony,
with its shards of *Sprechstimme*, the Ronettes, whatnot,
and in the air around us
something like the odor of a freshly spent cartridge,
when my minder asks brightly,
– *How about another Coke?*

September: Lake Wannsee, Berlin

I would rather have been Dufy
with these sails and darkening clouds –
well, not Dufy, and this is not *Le Sud*:
better, say, Cranach,
had he been given to painting sails
against the day's last light.
Perhaps there is a kind of sail in Mary's eyes,
poor thing.
                    The Baltic night is moving in,
dragging its somber quilt behind
like a filthy bridal train.
I would rather have enacted this in paint,
have the brushstrokes tell
what just passed through,
brightly at first
and then not, a glove of shadow across my sternum.

How much there is to know, to find,
should one step into the water and dive deep down
with a lamp and Baedeker,
a floor plan of the spirit museum
with its black onyx cloisters and galleries
that open one on the next
filled with jawbones, beetles, fiery gems,
tapestries almost water, immaterial,
bleeding signs.
                    Then set it down in paint,
the blacks, the greens and browns;
not explain.
Cumbersome words: imprecise, always hurrying
to catch up and never quite.
But further, further still:
even the painter must be destroyed
in order that one may become the paint.

The Tartar Swept

The Tartar swept across the plain
In their furs and silk panties
Snub-nosed monkey men with cinders for eyes
Attached to their ponies like centaurs
Forcing the snowy passes of the Carpathians
Streaming from defiles like columns of ants
Arraying their host in a vasty wheel
White, gray, black and chestnut steeds
10,000 each to a quadrant
Turning, turning at the Jenuye's command
This terrible pinwheel
Gathering speed like a Bulgar dance
Faster and faster
Until it explodes, columns of horsemen
Peeling away in all the four directions
Hard across the *puszta*
Dust from their hooves darkening the sky
They fall upon village and town
Like raptors, like tigers, like wolves on the fold
Mauling the *zsa-zsas*
And leaving them senseless in puddles of goaty drool
Smashing balalaikas
Ripping the ears off hussars and pissing in the wounds

They for whom the back of a horse

Is their only country

For whom a roof and four walls is like unto a grave

And a city, *ptuh*, a city

A pullulating sore that exists to be scourged

Stinky dumb nomads with blood still caked

On shield and cuirass

And the yellow loess from the dunes of the Takla Makan

And the corridor of Kansu

Between their toes and caught in their scalps

Like storm clouds in the distance

Fast approaching

With news of the steppes, the lagoons and Bitter Lakes

Edicts, torchings, infestation

The smoke of chronicles

Finding their way by the upper reaches

Of the Selinga and the Irtysh

To Issyk-Kul, the Aral, and then the Caspian

Vanquishing the Bashkirs and Alans

By their speed outstripping rumor

Tireless mounts, short-legged and strong

From whose backs arrows are expertly dispatched

As fast as they can be pulled from the quiver

Samarkand, Bukhara, Harat, Nishapur

More violent in every destruction

This race of men which had never before been seen

With their roving fierceness

Scarcely known to ancient documents

From beyond the edge of Scythia

From beyond the frozen ocean

Pouring out of the Caucasus

Surpassing every extreme of ferocity

From the Don to the Dniester

The Black Sea to the Pripet Marshes

Laying waste the Ostrogoth villages

Taking with them every last cookie

Then dicking the help

These wanton boys of nature

Who shot forward like a bolt from on high

Routing with great slaughter

All that they could come to grips with

In their wild career

Their beautiful shifting formations

Thousands advancing at the wave of a scarf

Then doubling back or making a turn

With their diabolical sallies and feints

Remorseless and in poor humor

So they arrived at the gates of Christendom